Napol

PATH TO PURPOSE

Napoleon Hill's

PATH TO PURPOSE

7 Steps to Living a Life that Matters

NAPOLEON HILL FOUNDATION

Published and distributed by:
SOUND WISDOM
P.O. Box 310
Shippensburg, PA 17257-0310
717-530-2122

info@soundwisdom.com

www.soundwisdom.com

ISBN 13 TP: 978-1-64095-465-6

ISBN 13 eBook: 978-1-64095-466-3

For Worldwide Distribution, Printed in the U.S.A.

1 2023

CONTENTS

PREFACE BY DON M. GREEN 9

INTRODUCTION 11

1 DETERMINE WHAT YOU MOST WANT FROM LIFE 15

2 DESIGN DEFINITE PLANS FOR ACHIEVING YOUR GOALS 29

3 STRENGTHEN YOUR PURPOSE WITH APPLIED FAITH 47

4 CULTIVATE THE ART OF ACCURATE THINKING 59

5 EXPRESS ORGANIZED THINKING THROUGH ACTION 71

6 SHARPEN YOUR FOCUS THROUGH CONTROLLED ATTENTION 83

7 HARNESS THE LAW OF HARMONIOUS ATTRACTION 95

CONCLUSION 103

MY PATH TO PURPOSE JOURNAL 107

ABOUT NAPOLEON HILL 125

If you haven't the strength to impose your own terms upon life, then you must accept the terms it offers you.

—T. S. ELIOT

PREFACE

BY DON M. GREEN

Executive Director and CEO of the Napoleon Hill Foundation

Famous author and speaker Napoleon Hill was addressing a dental convention in Chicago, Illinois, in 1952, and insurance tycoon W. Clement Stone, a longtime follower of Hill's teachings, was in attendance and introduced himself. At the time, Napoleon was sixty-nine years old, semiretired, and living happily with his wife, Annie Lou, in California, but Stone had an idea: he and Hill could go into business together and continue to spread the philosophy of success. Stone was persuasive and convinced Hill to come out of his semiretirement and resume writing and speaking under the auspices of the Napoleon Hill Associates, the organization they soon founded.

One of their first projects was putting together a lecture series focused on Hill's seventeen success principles that would be delivered in person to trainees who could then teach the success philosophy. The lectures were delivered in 1953 and thereafter were used as a basis for classroom instruction.

The lessons in this book derive from these never-before-published lectures. The principles presented here were selected to showcase the starting point of all achievement as explained by Hill, which is having a Definite Major Purpose. Put another way, he often said and wrote, "First, what do you want?" because without a definite goal, there can be no success. Without a major purpose, use of the other principles is unguided and ineffectual. Accordingly, the introduction of this book illuminates this fundamental success requisite, and the succeeding seven chapters detail principles as to how one can select, apply, and realize one's Definite Major Purpose, namely, creative vision, definite plans, applied faith, accurate thinking, self-discipline, controlled attention, and the law of harmonious attraction.

We believe you will enjoy the practical tips and philosophical insight contained in these pages on how to find purpose and focus in life. The ideas ring as true today as they did when the original lectures were delivered, in the middle of the last century. Napoleon Hill's success principles are ageless and eternal.

After you read this book and learn from it, we hope you will ask yourself, "First, what do you want?" Continue to read, study, and ponder the contents of this book, and you will be equipped not only to answer that question, but also to live it out.

DEFINITENESS OF PURPOSE

Definiteness of Purpose is the starting point of all achievement. Remember this statement because it is critical to your personal and professional happiness. There can be no success in any form whatsoever that does not begin with a *Definite Major Purpose*–a central motivation so specific, fixed, and vital that the pursuit of its object provides you with a sense of deep, abiding fulfillment and the ability to withstand temporary defeat. All riches–emotional, psychological, financial, material, and relational–are built on the foundation of Definiteness of Purpose.

If you were to gather together one hundred people, ninety-eight of them would lack this essential quality. Think of it! Ninety-eight percent of the people of the world have no idea what sort of work they are best suited for and what objective will inspire them to continually strive toward its attainment. They are perfectly fine with aimlessly drifting through life, struggling through their daily routine without a greater vision for their future. Every day is like the one before it: they rush from one task to the next in the hopes of making it through a to-do list that leads to nowhere in particular, all the while nursing a sinking feeling in the pit of their stomach that there must be more to life than just keeping busy. This is the fate of the vast majority of individuals because their actions are not backed by, or directed toward, a burning desire that has been solidified into a Definite Major Purpose. Indeed, only two out of every hundred have anything remotely akin to Definiteness of Purpose, and these are the ones who are succeeding because *they are not settling for anything short of what they want out of life.*

I hope that you will resolve from this day forward not to settle for anything short of what you want. Make a promise to yourself right now that you will get on a path to finding and living out your purpose so that you can live a life that fills you with a sense of significance. Will you do that? I am not just using empty words when I tell you that you don't have to settle for anything less than what you want. If you are really determined to get a thing, you can get it. Of course, if you don't have the ambition to start making life pay off on your own terms, there isn't anything that I or anyone else can do. But the fact that you are reading this book suggests that you have a fire in you waiting to be lit–a desire that, once awakened, will move you to greet each day with a firm sense of purpose and an appetite for achievement.

The steps outlined in this book chart the path to Definiteness of Purpose, but they also provide a roadmap to freedom. The philosophy of individual achievement from which they derive is a philosophy of human freedom and abundance. It is an antidote for poverty and want. Not only will it put you on the road to material and financial success, but it will give you a far greater gift of spiritual and mental freedom. For all these forms of riches—the tangible and the intangible alike—are found in the pursuit of a greater purpose that is firmly connected to one's unique skills, inclinations, and capabilities. Notice that I said the *pursuit* of a greater purpose. It is not in the attainment of a major goal but in the steadfast striving toward one that true freedom is found.

There are more opportunities for personal freedom now than at any other time in history, but it is up to you to take advantage of them by having a definite idea of what you want that will make you free and a definite plan by which you can attain your purpose. Freedom of body and mind requires very careful planning to achieve, and "few there be that find it." Many people, even those with plenty of money, bind themselves to too many "things" and fail to be really free. As you take steps toward realizing your purpose, remember that success is not an endpoint but a mindset. It is a state of mind in which you are in complete control of your thoughts so that you can avoid the traps of distraction, procrastination, fear, and negativity that every day will try to derail you from living out your purpose.

The wonderful reality is that this form of success is available to everyone. Every human being has the capacity to take complete control of their own mind. Indeed, thought is the *only* thing over which human beings have absolute control. Definiteness of Purpose is the first step toward attaining this mind control.

Your thinking makes you what you are and what you shall become. If the circumstances of your life are not to your liking, you may change them by changing your mental attitude to conform with the circumstances you desire. The seven steps outlined in this book will show you how to do just that by aligning your thoughts and actions with a Definite Major Purpose. As you apply each principle, you will clear out more and more of the undergrowth that shrouds your path to purpose so that you can move forward confidently on your journey to personal freedom, lasting success, and boundless contribution, *living a life that matters.*

CHAPTER 1

DETERMINE WHAT YOU MOST WANT FROM LIFE

The starting point of all individual achievement is the adoption of a Definite Major Purpose and a definite plan for its attainment. This chapter deals with the first component of this fundamental success formula: selecting a major purpose toward which your thoughts and efforts should be directed. Out of all the desires that swirl around in your mind, many of which are transient and forgotten almost as soon as they are formed, how do you know what you really want in life? And how can you be sure that what you want is worthy of your time and energy day after day, year after year–that it will lead to peace of mind and a lasting sense of fulfillment? While some of this requires faith, the principles in this chapter will help you cut through the noise, internal and external, that prevents so many of us from establishing a major purpose so that you can define yours, clearly and concisely, and start living it out now.

THE BENEFITS OF CHOOSING A DEFINITE MAJOR PURPOSE

Before we uncover the process of choosing a Definite Major Purpose in life, let us establish the many advantages of making up your mind.

1. Determining your major purpose will *enable you to develop several important qualities* that will enhance your ability to achieve your goals in life, such as:

- Self-reliance
- Personal initiative
- Imagination
- Enthusiasm
- Self-discipline
- Concentration of effort

2. Definiteness of Purpose *encourages you to specialize,* and specialization tends toward perfection. When you have found the right combination of your own basic aptitudes (physical and mental capacities) and desires (likes and dislikes) and the corresponding opportunity to utilize them, you should immediately begin to acquire specialized knowledge in your major field of interest (the things you most want to to). Definiteness of Purpose has a way of magnetizing

Definiteness of Purpose has a way of magnetizing the mind so as to attract to you the specialized knowledge necessary for success.

the mind so as to attract to you the specialized knowledge necessary for success.

3. Definiteness of Purpose will *induce you to budget your time and money* and to plan all of your day-to-day endeavors so that they lead to the attainment of your major purpose.

4. Definiteness of Purpose alerts the mind to opportunities and gives courage for action.

5. Definiteness of Purpose *helps you to develop the capacity to reach decisions quickly and firmly.* Successful people make decisions quickly–as soon as all the facts are available–and change them very slowly, if ever. Unsuccessful people make decisions very slowly and change them often and quickly. You can probably imagine the dire results of permitting indecision to leave you "forever on the fence," letting others do your thinking for you.

6. Establishing a Definite Major Purpose *inspires the cooperation of others.* Conditioning your mind with a clear, firm purpose will send signals to those in your vicinity, causing them to pick up the signals subconsciously and act in accordance with the positive suggestions they contain. That is why those individuals who know where they are going and are determined to get there will always find willing helpers along the way.

7. Definiteness of Purpose *prepares the mind for faith.* It makes the mind positive and frees it from the limitations of fear, doubt, discouragement, indecision, and procrastination. Doubt usually results in alibis, excuses, and apologies for failure.

8. Finally, choosing your major purpose *provides you with a success consciousness.* Your mind becomes "sold" on succeeding and refuses to accept the possibility of failing.

HOW TO IDENTIFY YOUR DEFINITE MAJOR PURPOSE

Now that we have surveyed the many benefits of identifying your Definite Major Purpose, let us discuss how to pinpoint this most crucial objective. Start by asking yourself: *What do I most desire from life*? That is something you and *you alone* can decide. This major purpose might be likened to a blueprint you are drawing of your entire future life, including every single element you can possibly anticipate as an object of your desire at this time. It might include different combinations of lesser or minor aims, such as, for instance:

- The nature of your occupation, which should be something of your own choosing.

- The amount of your weekly, monthly, or yearly income, which should be enough to enable you to enjoy a standard of life that you have chosen and to provide for sickness, accidents, old age, and the loss of earning power.
- A plan for developing and maintaining harmony in all of your human relationships–in your home, at your work, where you play and relax. Human relationships are vital to your aim in life because you must have the cooperation of others in order to achieve any success above mediocrity.

To help you brainstorm, try writing your major purpose as though you were penning a letter to a friend, explaining what it is you most want to do in life. Include details such as:

- The objectives you want to attain
- The information or knowledge you want to acquire
- The kind of work you want to do
- The kind of person you want to be–your personality, character, and other relevant traits
- How much you want to earn and receive each year
- The places you want to visit and see
- The skills, arts, crafts, and sciences you wish to master

From this letter, extract the key details about your major purpose and organize them into categories. Create a table with five headings: Vocation, Personal Growth, Home and Family Life, Spiritual Enlightenment, and Social Responsibilities. List the various details you pulled out from your letter under the heading to which it most closely relates.

From there, circle the elements and ideas that are non-negotiables for you–that are integral to your vision of success and significance, however you define these intangibles.

This exercise should help you drill down to the most crucial elements of your Definite Major Purpose, which you should now be able to format as a clear concise statement. Consider using the following template:

> I will accomplish ____________________ by the date of _____________. I want to direct all my energy and effort toward reaching this major goal because ___________________________. And I am willing to give __________________ in return for achieving this life purpose.

Be specific; be definite–for if your aims in life are vague, your achievements will also be vague (and likely very meager as well). Know what you want, when you want it, why you want it, and *how* you intend to get it. And don't forget to acknowledge the cost of what realizing your major goal will likely require–for nothing worth doing in life comes without a price, whether that be in time, money, or other tradeoffs.

If your aims in life are vague, your achievements will also be vague.

EXPLORING YOUR PURPOSE THROUGH CREATIVE VISION

The imagination is a powerful tool for enriching your understanding of your major purpose in life. Imagination, or creative vision, may be an inborn quality of the mind, or it may be an acquired quality, for it may be developed by the free and fearless use of the faculty of imagination.

Surely, no one would claim that Thomas A. Edison was born with the inherent quality of genius, for if that had been true, why was he sent home from school after only three months of common school training with a note from his teacher saying that he had an addled mind and therefore could not benefit from an education? And why did he flounder around from one job to another before he found himself?

No, Edison was not born a genius. He became a genius by the inspiration of motives that caused him to take an inventory of himself, to make up his mind what he desired most to do, and then to start, right where he stood, doing just that.

Edison's creative vision was the product of his own mind, and it was of his own making! The same may be said of Henry Ford and Andrew Carnegie and of all the other great American leaders whom most of us have learned to respect because of their contributions to the American way of life.

One of the common weaknesses of most of us consists in the fact that we look with envy at the people who have attained noteworthy success, taking stock of them during the hour of their triumph without taking note of the price each had to pay for his or her success. And we erroneously believe that they owe their success to some sort of luck, connection, or dishonesty.

Personal achievement has a definite price, and those individuals with creative vision not only know the price but are willing to pay it! They explore, test, and refine their burning desires until they have honed in on a clear purpose whose achievement will bring them the riches (material or otherwise) they most desire and serve others in some way.

A TEST FOR YOUR DEFINITE MAJOR PURPOSE

You might be asking yourself, *How can I be sure that the Definite Major Purpose I have chosen for myself is worthwhile?* A test of whether the purpose you now have in mind is worthy of being a major purpose involves asking yourself the following questions:

- *Am I willing to spend most of my lifetime making it come true?*
- *Will it be worth the price I may have to pay for it?*
- *Will attaining it benefit others beyond myself?*

If the answer to all three questions is a resounding "yes," then it is a goal worthy of the commitment required for a Definite Major Purpose. If you cannot be certain on these three points, consider spending more time reflecting on what lights you up in life and how that might be channeled into a purpose that leads to success, significance, and impact.

If you are not accustomed to setting goals and achieving them, and if you are not accustomed to long-range planning, start out with a minor, but important, purpose. Set up a purpose that must be accomplished, say, in six months or a year from now. Then, as it is achieved, set yourself another higher more difficult and longer-range objective, thus growing into the habit before setting down your major purpose for a lifetime.

Once you establish this rhythm of habit formation and achievement, return to the exercises in this chapter to see whether you can get any closer to determining your Definite Major Purpose. When you are able to articulate your major purpose in a clear, concise statement, write it down on a card that you can carry with you. Read this statement of your Definite Major Purpose aloud to yourself once each morning and each night, at the very least, until you have memorized it. Call it to mind every time you possibly can. In the repetition of your purpose, emotionalize each item and visualize the benefits that will accrue to you and all others concerned in its fulfillment.

Determining your Definite Major Purpose is the most critical step on the path to individual achievement. Take your time in identifying your major purpose, for while plans might change, your purpose should not–at least, not substantially. It might get refined, but it should be your North Star that guides all your actions.

Determining your Definite Major Purpose is the most critical step on the path to individual achievement.

And remember that purpose without action is completely ineffectual. As Andrew Carnegie said: "The way of success is the way of action"–action grounded in Definiteness of Purpose. With that in mind, we turn next to the formation of a definite plan, which is how our thoughts and actions must be expressed in order to attain the object of our major purpose.

CHAPTER 2

DESIGN DEFINITE PLANS FOR ACHIEVING YOUR GOALS

As you learned in the previous chapter, every achievement, regardless of its size, begins with a Definite Major Purpose *and* a definite plan for its attainment. A purpose without any action backing it is only a wish. Wishing, in reality, is merely a form of procrastination.

A Definite Major Purpose is a goal so strong and specific that it incites you to take action toward its realization every day. But in order for this action to be constructive, you must define your path–your *plan*. Planning ensures that your actions are aligned to support your goal achievement, and it enables you to enlist the support of others to accelerate your progress. The first step toward crafting an impactful plan for attaining the object of your Definite Major Purpose is determining which motive or combination of motives will fuel your actions.

SELECT THE RIGHT MOTIVES

Some people confuse motives with purpose, but you are not one of those people. You know that motives are based on emotions and desires, whereas purpose is a definite goal toward which you are striving. One is a feeling; the other is as close to a fact as it comes. Your Definite Major Purpose is your truth–the goal whose realization demands every ounce of your natural talents, skills, and self-discipline. But don't discount emotions–in order to achieve your major purpose, you need to identify the right set of motives to back your actions. Having a burning desire behind your major purpose is essential, and you are not going to have a burning desire unless you have a motive that emotionally sets you on fire.

There are nine basic motives that inform all actions:

1. The *emotion of love*, of which there are several types: love of truth or principle, which is the highest form of love; romantic love, which involves the ingredients of physical attraction, affection, and intellectual and spiritual companionship; love of neighbor, which includes parental love, love of other family members, friends, etc.; a labor of love, which is a deep enjoyment of work such that it brings forth your best creative effort; and self-love.

2. The *emotion of sex*, which, when channeled toward a higher aim, can inspire true genius.

3. The *desire for material gain*, which is more effective when you focus not on the mere possession of material riches but rather the good you can do with them.

4. The *desire for self-preservation*, as nothing will make an individual strive harder and connect more deeply with their "other self"–the self within whose resolve is so strong it will overcome any challenge–than facing hunger or some other threat to their basic needs.

5. The *desire for freedom of body and mind*, for the ability to live and work on your own schedule, in your own way, is the reason many set large goals for themselves.

6. The *desire for self-expression and recognition*, which compels many to direct their talents and skills toward the achievement of a major objective.

7. The *desire for life after death*, as leaving a legacy motivates many to pursue greatness.

8. The *desire for revenge*, a negative motive that, while powerful, can backfire. Nothing leads to failure more readily than trying to deprive someone else of that which is rightfully theirs.

9. The *emotion of fear*, another destructive motive that can take on a life of its own if not kept in check. In order to succeed in your aims, you must take control

> of the powers of your mind and keep them focused in a positive manner upon the object of your desire.

These nine motives constitute the "alphabet of success," ensuring you remain committed to achieving your goals. They also enable you to interact more effectively with other people, for all people engage in voluntary action because of a motive.

Take time now to consider which motive or combination of motives will keep you committed to working toward your Definite Major Purpose, even (or especially) on the toughest days.

ACTIVATE THE SUBCONSCIOUS MIND

Having a strong motive or set of motives will not only keep you engaged in the pursuit of your Definite Major Purpose, but it will also activate the subconscious mind to help you determine the best plan for the realization of this purpose. While nobody really knows much about how the subconscious mind works, we do know that there is some element in the mind that acts very similarly to the sensitized film in a camera.

any image that is transferred to it by the conscious mind under the influence of a strong emotion. The conscious mind acts as the "lens" of the mental camera. It collects the light rays reflected by the object of your desire and brings them to a focal point. Getting good pictures with this camera is like getting them with any other: the focus must be sharp, there must be good exposure,

These nine motives constitute the "alphabet of success," ensuring you remain committed to achieving your goals.

There is some element in the mind that acts very similarly to the sensitized film in a camera.

and the timing must be right. Correct focus means getting a clear definition of the object–that's Definiteness of Purpose. The arrangement or composition of the picture must be made with care and precision, and the elements must be sharply defined; in other words, you must know the size, shape, color, texture, value, and quantity of whatever it is you want, if it is something material, and the equivalent of these qualities if it is something intangible.

When you have a vivid image in your conscious mind (the lens), and when you relate all of the elements in your dream picture to one or more of the nine basic motives, this motivation will enable you to create a burning desire. While under this emotion, you will be able to transfer the image to your subconscious mind (the film) in all of its original brilliance and detail. The "timing" varies with the intensity of your desire when the "exposure" is made, and in this particular type of camera, several "shots" may be needed before the picture is fully developed. When the picture transfers successfully to your subconscious mind, it will partner with your imagination to generate the best plan for achieving your major goal.

SIT FOR IDEAS

Now that you have the right motive or set of motives to emotionalize your Definite Major Purpose, giving it vividness and urgency within the subconscious mind, it is time to start working out a plan for the realization of your objective. All plans begin with an idea–and it takes only one good idea to attain the success you desire.

Did you know that ideas are what make the world go around? Ideas are the only assets that have no fixed values. And ideas are the beginning of all achievements. Ideas emerge as the result of Definiteness of Purpose. The most important part of this book is not written on these pages–*it is already in your own mind!* The lessons in this book will teach you how to harness the stupendous potential power of your own mind and organize the knowledge you already have and turn it into the power necessary for the development and attainment of your major purpose in life.

There are two main ways that the mind can work out a plan for your success–either using the *creative imagination* or the *synthetic imagination.* With the creative imagination, your subconscious mind partners with Infinite Intelligence to generate a completely new idea. This entirely original thought comes as a flash of inspiration or a "hunch," as if placed in the mind by an external force.

The more common type of creative thinking involves the synthetic imagination, by which existing ideas are rearranged or recontextualized to produce new combinations. The invention of the Piggly Wiggly supermarket chain is an excellent study in the value of the synthetic imagination. In Memphis, Tennessee, a young man at lunchtime stood gazing at a long line of patrons in a newly established cafeteria, waiting their turn, with trays in hand, to serve themselves. Curiosity inspired him to join the line

Ideas are the beginning of all achievements.

and find out how the new system worked. As he placed his last dish on his tray, his curiosity began to manifest itself in the form of imagination.

By the time he had finished his meal, his imagination had conceived an idea that was destined to greatly improve his finances. The idea was not new, for it consisted of the self-service system he had just seen in operation, but it was moved by the aid of his imagination to a new setting and a new use. He reasoned that the self-service system would go well in the grocery business, and he promptly put that idea into action by creating the first Piggly Wiggly grocery store. The first store was followed by others until the Piggly Wiggly chain was in operation throughout many of the United States. In the first four years of operation, the stores were so successful that Saunders sold the business for $4,000,000, thus receiving a million dollars a year for giving an established idea a new use! The time necessary to create that idea was less than an hour, but it was the most profitable time of Saunders's life.

Sometimes we hinder our own progress because we are convinced that we need an entirely new idea, but *there is real power in repurposed ideas.* Do not limit yourself to the creative imagination; instead, consider how you might breathe new life into ideas that others have tried and discarded or simply rework a successful idea into a different version that aids you in your purpose.

Activating the imagination to lead us to the right plan for our purpose requires us to cultivate awareness, both internal and external. Dr. Elmer R. Gates, a scientist and great inventor who

Activating the imagination to lead us to the right plan for our purpose requires us to cultivate awareness, both internal and external.

was a contemporary of Thomas A. Edison, had a unique method for tuning out noise (within and without) and tuning in to his surroundings and his subconscious to locate ideas for how to accomplish his aims. I refer to this method as "the habit of sitting for ideas," for that is precisely what he did. For this purpose, he had a sound-proof room in which he did the "sitting." When he desired the solution of a problem, he went into this room, closed the door, seated himself at a table supplied with pencil and paper, and turned off the lights. Then he concentrated his thoughts upon the nature of his problem and waited for the reception of ideas that he needed for its solution.

Sometimes the ideas would immediately begin flowing into his mind. At other times, he waited for an hour or more before they began to make their appearance. And on some occasions, no ideas came through, but such occasions were rare. By this method, Dr. Gates refined and perfected more than 250 patents, some covering ideas that other inventors with weaker imaginations had undertaken to perfect–without success. He added to their ideas the finishing touch that was needed to give them mechanical perfection.

CRAFT A PLAN

Whether you "sit for ideas" or gather them piece by piece, at some point you must assemble them into a written plan. The temptation exists to form and hold the plan in your mind rather than write it down; however, it is crucial that you commit your plan to writing so that, through writing, you imprint it onto your subconscious mind, as well as have a written guide to which you can regularly refer.

Write out a definite, clear, concise plan by which you intend to achieve your Definite Major Purpose. Include the following details:

1. State the maximum amount of time you are allowing for the fulfillment of your desire.
2. Break the achievement down into units of effort that are in the realm of possibility and probability. What do you intend to complete this month? In six months' time? What about by the end of the year? In five, ten, or more years? Be bold and confident in your intentions, but keep them within the bounds of what you can reasonably accomplish on your own or with the assistance of others.
3. Whose talent, time, influence, and/or resources will you require to attain the object of your desire? Be as specific as possible, also noting when you will reach out to these individuals for their support.
4. It is important that you describe precisely what you intend to give in return for the realization of your purpose.

Don't let planning turn into a façade for procrastination.

Make your plan flexible so as to permit changes. Your Definite Major Purpose, if it really is that, will not change until it is fulfilled, but the plan for achieving that purpose may change many times.

Keep your Definite Major Purpose and your plans for achievement strictly to yourself. Do not talk about them or tell anyone about them, except the members of your mastermind alliance.

Remember to call your major purpose and your plans into your consciousness as often as may be practical. *Keep your mind on the things you want and off the things you don't want.*

START BEFORE YOUR PLAN IS READY

Your plan will take time to develop, and even after you create it there will be times when you will have to refine it, or perhaps even discard it altogether in favor of another one. If you wait until your plan is "perfect" to take action, then you will never make progress on attaining the object of your major purpose. Andrew Carnegie recognized the perils of deferred action when explained:

> If a man wishes to do something, he should start right where he stands and begin doing it. But most men will say, "What shall I use for tools? Where will I get the working capital needed? Who will help me?" My reply is that men who accomplish anything worthy of mention usually begin before everything they

> need is at hand. I have never yet been entirely ready for anything that I have undertaken, and I doubt if anyone else ever has been. It is one of the strangest phenomena of human experience that the man who begins where he stands, and does the best he can with whatever means may be available to him, very soon finds other and better means of accomplishing his objectives. Mysteriously the necessary tools, opportunities, and the help of others are placed at his disposal, in one way or another.
>
> The complaint so many men offer, of not being ready, usually is only an alibi with which they deceive no one except themselves. The lifetime if the average person is short at best. Time goes by in a hurry, and the man who does not embrace every second of his portion of it, and use it beneficially, will be left in the shuffle of the competitive circumstances of life. Decisions have to be made, objectives have to be chosen, plans have to be created for the attainment of objectives, and the man who hesitates when he has all of the necessary facts at hand to enable him to make a decision, will never get anywhere.

Don't let planning turn into a façade for procrastination. Gather the knowledge that you can to make an initial plan founded upon accurate thinking, even if you can identify only the first few steps that you should take. You will probably never feel that you are completely ready to start any project. There will always be something else you could do in preparation for your "take off." But you should start where you stand, work with whatever tools you have at hand, and other and better ones will reveal themselves to you as you move forward. Make one step forward and try out your present equipment. Implementing a preliminary plan will enable you to test its soundness and cultivate your personal initiative so that you maintain a habit of decisiveness and action. The positive momentum that results will work in your favor as you attempt to attain your Definite Major Purpose.

CHAPTER 3

STRENGTHEN YOUR PURPOSE WITH APPLIED FAITH

When we first form our definite major purpose, we often feel so sure about it–positive that it is the highest realization of our dreams, skills, and talents; certain that we can do what we need to do to achieve it. But when it comes time to take action toward a smaller goal on the path toward our major purpose, we find ourselves faltering. We begin to doubt our ability to succeed in our aims. And worse–we begin to doubt our purpose. To keep ourselves on the road to success, we need to back our purpose with an unshakeable faith in our ability to achieve it. Thankfully, faith is not a feeling we passively receive; it is a state of mind we can–and must–actively cultivate.

THE BATTLE BETWEEN FEAR AND FAITH

There are two mental states in which we form our thoughts and convert them into actions: fear and faith. Fear is a state of mind that encompasses the emotions of doubt, worry, and discouragement. Faith is a force created by self-confidence, belief, optimism, and enthusiasm. These two states are constantly at war with each other, except for the individual who has taken complete control of their own mind and forced the evil influences out of it.

The emotion of fear and the emotion of faith are so unfriendly that both cannot possibly occupy the mind of a person at the same time. One or the other must dominate, always. Too often it is the negative emotion of fear that comes out the winner.

There are six basic fears that weaken your certainty of purpose and lead to procrastination, indecision, and a general posture of doubt:

- Fear of poverty
- Fear of criticism
- Fear of ill health
- Fear of loss of love
- Fear of old age
- Fear of death

Each of these fears is like a weed–when it takes root in the garden of your mind, it begins to crowd out the buds of hope and faith. As with a physical garden, you do not have to water the weeds for them to grow; they will sprout and flourish as a result of inattention. Without your guidance, nature plants all the things you *don't want*, but you can plant the seeds of the things

Nature plants all the things you ***don't want,*** *but you can plant the seeds of the things you desire.*

you desire, and nature will be just as bountiful in producing the things you *do want.*

Self-suggestion is the technique through which you may voluntarily feed your subconscious mind thoughts of a creative nature or, by neglect, permit thoughts of a destructive nature to find your way into this rich garden. Definiteness of Purpose will keep your mind clear of the things you don't want and keep it so busy working on the things you do want that it will have no time to grow weeds–undesired things. Without tending to your mental garden, the weeds of fear and doubt will overtake your mind until you are left with a mindset of failure consciousness.

Thankfully, you have complete control over the thoughts that occupy your mind. You have all the tools you need to create the mental conditions necessary for success consciousness; primary among these is faith.

Weed out the seeds of fear through the power of *decision.* Disempower your fears by taking away their emotional force and creating new mental habits centered on faith. Self-discipline is critical here: refusing to give your fears the emotional weight they demand and taking positive action in spite of them *requires nothing but a daily decision to be governed by faith* rather than fear. You must be intentional about monitoring the thoughts that go in and out of your mind and committed to doing work every day in service of your major purpose.

Discouragement and doubt are the keenest tools in the "devil's" toolkit. When you allow indecision to leave you "forever on the fence," letting others do your thinking, you permit others to dictate how you understand and act (or rather don't act) on your purpose. Procrastination is another deadly form of this same weakness, and it can be overcome only with faith, persistence, and strict self-discipline. Inaction and passive thinking breed doubt and fear; focused, positive thinking and constructive action breed faith and success.

THE SELF-CONFIDENCE FORMULA

Faith strengthens our resolve in our major purpose, and it is also the natural outgrowth of a purpose that is characterized by definiteness. In other words, we can apply faith to our purpose to solidify it, and we can develop more belief around our purpose by sharpening our vision of it.

The greatest of all the benefits of *definiteness* of purpose is that it opens the way for the full exercise of that state of mind known as FAITH. Through the application of faith, your mind becomes "sold" on succeeding and refuses to accept the possibility of failing. It makes the mind positive and frees it from the limitations of fear, doubt, discouragement, indecision, and procrastination. Doubt usually results in alibis, excuses, and apologies for failure. Remember:

"SUCCESS REQUIRES NO EXPLANATION—FAILURE PERMITS NO ALIBIS."

Through the application of faith, your mind becomes "sold" on succeeding and refuses to accept the possibility of failing.

To cultivate Definiteness of Purpose, implement the following formula on a daily basis:

1. Believe in your ability to achieve the object of your Definite Major Purpose, and demand of yourself persistent, continuous action toward its attainment.

2. Concentrate your thoughts for thirty minutes daily on the person you intend to become.

3. Apply the principle of *autosuggestion* by dedicating ten minutes each day to the task of focusing your thoughts on your desire to develop self-confidence.

4. Write down a clear description of your Definite Major Purpose in life, and never stop trying to attain it.

5. Commit to never engaging in any action that is not founded upon truth and justice. Reject all thoughts of hatred, envy, jealousy, selfishness, and cynicism, and cultivate a love for all humanity, recognizing that a negative attitude toward others will never bring you success. Not only will this inspire self-confidence, but it will cause others to believe in your purpose and want to contribute toward its attainment.

By following these steps, the power made available by the subconscious mind is stimulated and amplified by the power of FAITH. A force is created that accepts no such reality as the possibility of failure. This constitutes genius, and genius that may be developed by any person!

THE POWER OF APPLIED FAITH

It is important to pause here and distinguish between faith in the abstract and Applied Faith. The former is a pleasant emotion that can support the development of a positive mental attitude, a necessary ingredient for success consciousness and for enlisting the cooperation of others to carry out our plans. However, only Applied Faith–faith that is concentrated upon the attainment of your Definite Major Purpose–will translate your thoughts about realizing your purpose into the actual attainment of this purpose. That is, you cannot put forward merely a "blanket" faith, some vague belief in yourself and the positive things to come in your life; you must cultivate a specific belief in your ability to live out your purpose.

How do you do this? Through daily *application*. Those individuals who have adopted a Definite Major Purpose and are actively engaged in carrying out the object of their purpose thereby demonstrate their faith in their ability to attain their objective.

Thoughts, backed by faith and characterized be definiteness, have precedence over all others in the speed with which they are handed over to the subconscious mind and acted upon. Faith plays the role of an accelerator, which can speed up the reaction

You must cultivate a specific belief in your ability to live out your purpose.

between the conscious and the subconscious mind. It is a known fact that individuals who are capable of freeing their mind from all self-imposed limitations (which is all that Applied Faith actually is) generally find the solution to all of their problems regardless of their nature. Such individuals don't know what's "impossible," so they go ahead and do it.

So go ahead and weed out any doubts, fears, or distractions that are poisoning your conception of your purpose and hindering your ability to live it out. Create mental habits that are conducive not just to inspiring a general faith, but to producing Applied Faith, which bolsters your resolve in your Definite Major Purpose. You will know, by your own state of mind, when the habit has become properly fixed, for then you will experience a continuous feeling of enthusiasm in connection with your plans, and you will be guided by a definite feeling of faith in your ability to achieve their object.

This enthusiasm will inspire you to action during your every conscious moment, and it will inspire you, through the subconscious section of your mind, while you sleep. You need not be surprised when your subconscious mind awakens you from sleep with an idea or a plan that will be useful in carrying out the object of your aims and purposes, for this has been the experience of many persons who jointly exercise Applied Faith and Definiteness of Purpose. You will attain a heightened emotional state that we associate with "spiritual power."

As Andrew Carnegie explains: "When one's mind is stimulated by this exalted feeling, the faculty of his imagination becomes more alert, his words take on a more magnetic tone which makes them more impressive, fear and self-imposed limitations disappear and he dares to undertake tasks he would not think of beginning when his mind is stimulated only by the purely mental process of thinking."

Gradually, the dark glasses of despair you may have been wearing will change their color, and you will begin to see the world around you through crystal clear glasses of hope and faith, for you will have changed the entire tempo of vibration of your being.

CHAPTER 4

CULTIVATE THE ART OF ACCURATE THINKING

The power of thought is the only thing over which any human being has complete, unquestionable control.

This statement is so critical to your present and future success that it bears repeating: the power of thought is the only thing over which any human being has complete, unquestionable control.

No matter how much you *want* to achieve your major purpose in life, no matter how much you *plan* for its attainment, you will never get anywhere close to success if you do not master your thoughts. Every person who achieves any form of enduring success above mediocrity must learn the art of thinking accurately. And Accurate Thinking is indeed an art–one not practiced by the vast majority of the population.

Most people do not think, other than just to think that they think!

The power of thought is the only thing over which any human being has complete, unquestionable control.

The mind is eternally at work, building up or tearing down, bringing misery, unhappiness, and poverty–or joy, pleasure, and riches. It is never idle!

It is the greatest of all the assets available to humankind, but it is the least used and the most abused of all assets. Its abuse consists mainly in its non-use.

It is impossible to attain the object of your major purpose without Accurate Thinking, which prevents you from getting led astray by every little challenge or difference in opinion. Accurate Thinking enables you to back your purpose with the full power of logic so that you are not swayed by emotion to change your path or slow your progress.

THE FUNDAMENTALS OF ACCURATE THINKING

Anyone can learn the art of Accurate Thinking; in fact, it takes self-training to become practiced in it. Our default state is not thinking accurately, as we are prone to be ruled by our emotions. We must bring these emotions under the control of our logical mind if we are to achieve the success we desire.

Accurate Thinking is based upon two major fundamentals:

- *Inductive reasoning*, based on the assumption of unknown facts or hypotheses
- *Deductive reasoning*, based on known facts, or what are believed to be facts

With inductive reasoning, you study several related examples or amass a set of observations and draw from them a general rule or hypothesis. Deductive reasoning works in the opposite direction: you begin with a principle or hypothesis that is believed to be true and apply it to specific instances. Both of these modes of reasoning will support you as you identify your purpose and pursue its realization.

While emotions can provide momentum to your goal achievement and raise the vibration of your thought to a level that activates the subconscious mind to work in your favor, they are only constructive if they are (1) of a positive nature and (2) kept under the control of the logical mind.

Most so-called thinking is nothing but an expression of feeling, through the emotions. And the emotions are not dependable. Accurate thinkers always submit their emotional desires and decisions to their head for thoughtful examination before they rely upon them as being sound, for they know that the head is more dependable than the heart.

The following emotions make Accurate Thinking impossible:

- Fear
- Love
- Anger
- Jealousy
- Revenge
- Vanity
- Greed

If you find yourself being driven by one of the above emotions, you can use a simple test for ensuring you are keeping yourself grounded in logic and rationality.

A SIMPLE TEST FOR ACCURATE THINKING

The first question you should ask yourself to ensure you are thinking accurately is the following: *Is it true?*

Inductive and deductive logic are the keys to helping you answer this question, as they will enable you to filter out the incorrect and baseless ideas that can hinder your progress.

Be wary, too, of other people's *opinions*, which might as well be understood as emotions that are cloaked in the guise of truth. Everyone but the accurate thinker has an overabundance of opinions. The vast majority of the time, opinions are without value, and many of them are dangerous and destructive in connection with your quest for success because most of them are based on bias, prejudice, intolerance, ignorance, guesswork, and hearsay evidence.

No opinion is sound unless it is based upon known facts, and no one should express an opinion on any subject without reasonable assurance that it is founded on facts or reasonable hypotheses of facts. Free advice volunteered by friends and acquaintances usually is not worthy of consideration. The accurate thinker, therefore, never acts upon such advice without giving it the closest scrutiny.

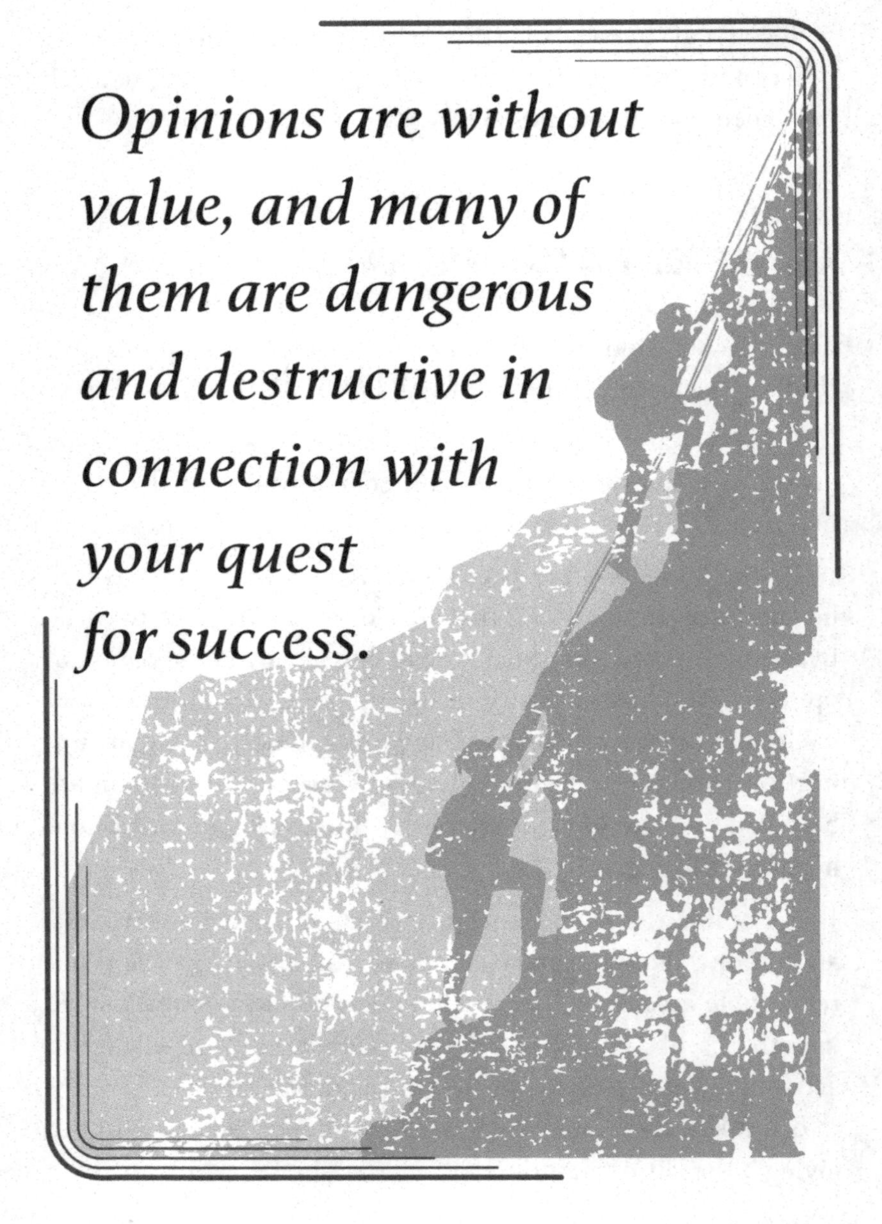

Opinions are without value, and many of them are dangerous and destructive in connection with your quest for success.

"Opinions" are plentiful. Everyone has a stock of them, but most of them are not only worthless, but they are dangerous as well, for they have not been acquired by the principle of Accurate Thinking. And that is true of many "opinions" that we embrace. At first we may not accept the opinion as being sound, but close association with it gradually influences us to endure it, then to embrace it as our own, often forgetting the source from which it came. How many so-called facts have we internalized because we surrounded ourselves with them for so long that we eventually equated repetition with truth?

The favorite question of accurate thinkers is "How do you know?" They demand to know the source of all that is presented to them as facts. They demand evidence of the soundness of these so-called facts. They know that anything that exists as a fact is capable of proof.

Accurate thinkers also take into consideration the motive of those sharing information with them. They probe into the source by exploring whether there is a profit interest or some other form of self-interest involved.

Furthermore, they assess the credibility of the source: Is the person sharing the information cool and collected or are they overzealous? A zealot is ruled by unchecked emotion and so cannot be trusted as a reliable source. Is the source a recognized authority? Can their statements be supported by verifiable sources?

Accurate thinkers learn to use their own judgment and to be cautious, no matter who may endeavor to influence them. If a statement does not harmonize with their own reasoning power, or if it is not in harmony with their experience, they hold it in abeyance for further examination. They put it through trials of inductive and deductive reasoning, talk it through with their mastermind group to ensure any inaccuracies or biases are filtered out.

Another common weakness in the habits of thought of most people consists in their tendency toward unbelief in everything they do not understand. Disbelief can be caught just as easily as belief in incorrect theories and destructive ideas.

Accurate thinkers permit no one to do their thinking for them! They often obtain facts, information, and counsel from others, but they retain for themselves the privilege of acceptance or rejection of any or all of these factors. They never count the media or the gossipers and scandalmongers as reliable sources. They do not invite advice from others as to their definite purpose or plan–even family members or those close to them. They seek out only the counsel of their mastermind group. Finally, accurate thinkers recognize that wishes are often untethered to facts; facts don't necessarily harmonize to wishes. For this reason, they can separate desire from truth, emotion from logic.

But factual information alone will not get you to your Definite Major Purpose. Accurate Thinking has a second ingredient–not only truth, but *relevance*. Therefore, the second question you must answer in order to protect your Definiteness of Purpose is this: *Is it important?*

Accurate thinkers permit no one to do their thinking for them!

What is an important fact? It is any fact that can be used to advantage in the attainment of your major purpose.

And what is an important fact? It is any fact that can be used to advantage in the attainment of your major purpose. All other facts are relatively unimportant. To stay focused on your major purpose, you must learn to tune in to those facts that are most useful to your definite chief aim. Otherwise, you will be prone to getting led astray on tangents of thought that impede your success.

If there is one portion of this success philosophy I am presenting which is more profound than any other it is the portion which I am now presenting, for we are dealing with the source of the real power behind all human achievements; the power which is responsible (through its misuse because of our ignorance) for much of the misery of mankind; the power which brings success or failure, according to the way it is applied.

CHAPTER 5

EXPRESS ORGANIZED THINKING THROUGH ACTION

Ordinary thought is not enough to ensure success. If it were sufficient, then every hope and wish would become a reality. In order to actualize your purpose, you must use Organized Thinking.

Thought is the master of all other forms of energy because it is a form of energy that is mixed with intelligence. Thought holds the solution to every human problem. It is the master of poverty and misery and worry and fear.

When it is properly used, its therapeutic powers are without limitation. Thought is the source of all riches, whether they be material, physical or spiritual riches, for it is the means by which all the riches of life may be appropriated by all who desire them.

Yet thought is of little benefit in connection with the accumulation of riches until it is organized and directed to definite ends through Definiteness of Purpose. Like electricity, thought is a power that can, and often does, destroy as readily as it constructs, if it is not controlled and applied to proper ends.

For this reason, Andrew Carnegie refers to thought as *mental dynamite.* It can be organized and used constructively for the attainment of definite ends, but if it is not controlled and directed in constructive ways, it may become a "mental explosive" that will literally blast your hopes of achievement and lead to inevitable failure.

A Definite Major Purpose is the key to organizing your thought power and expressing it through action.

THOUGHT = MENTAL DYNAMITE.

DISORGANIZED THOUGHTS PRODUCE HAPHAZARD RESULTS

The majority of individuals today "manage by crisis." That is, when things have drifted along to a point where something simply must be done, they make some temporary arrangement to bridge the gap and then crawl back into the comfortable rut of procrastination.

I could take you into the office of a man who is quite well known in the community and show you his desk. In one corner, there is an accumulation of magazines published for practitioners of his

The majority of individuals today "manage by crisis."

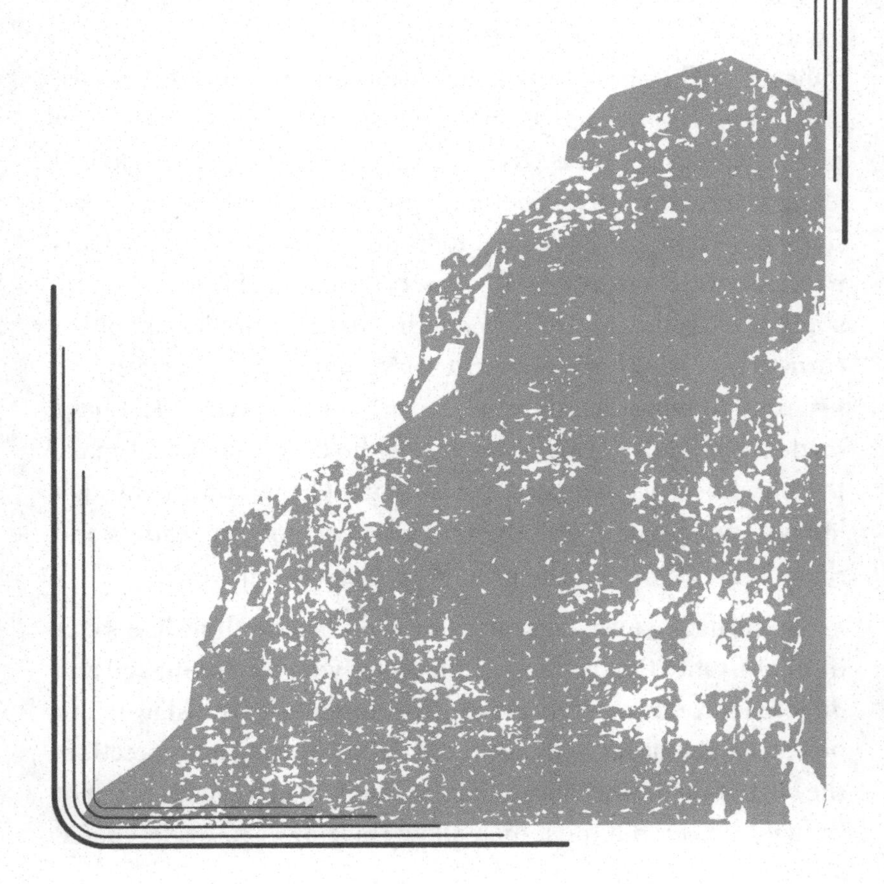

trade, dating back for months. They contain articles he's going to read "someday." In another corner, there is a pile approximately a foot high of letters, file folders, ragged newspaper clippings, and other pieces of scratch paper with notes on them, which are the basis of a proposed advertising campaign that has been "hanging fire" for nearly two years and is no nearer to actual adoption and carrying out than it was then.

This man is supposed to be an executive of a municipal utility, and he earns a very modest sum entirely because his desk is indicative of his mind in general. He has never been able to make a decision. He is reactive to situations that need his attention rather than being proactive. That is, when things have drifted along to a point where something simply must be done, he makes some temporary arrangement to bridge the gap and then crawls back into the comfortable rut of procrastination. From long-time study of this man's mind, I know that he is mentally capable of earning several times his present salary, but he will not discipline his mind to make decisions when the facts are available. I have made a big point of this because it is the little things that make the big difference between the ninety-eight who drift through life without purpose and the two who become the leaders and the doers and who set the pace of progress in our world.

As Carnegie says: "Organized thought is something like water in a dam. Only that portion of the water which is harnessed and directed through machinery, which is designed to translate it into power, can be of service. Without this harnessing and direction, the water only flows back to the sea. Every man has a reservoir of thought power, but most men allow this power to be dissipated through idle dreaming, never taking the trouble to organize it and direct it to definite ends. Like the water in a dam, it flows out without producing any useful action."

The most successful individuals in society earned their status by organizing their thoughts according to the nature of their Definite Major Purpose and expressing their thoughts through action. Either consciously or unconsciously these individuals gave orders to their minds to produce definite ends (the principle of Definiteness of Purpose), and their minds responded. "Genius" had nothing whatsoever to do with their achievements or, if it did, then every normal person is a genius, for anyone may produce such "miracles" by the simple process of taking possession of their own mind and directing it to definite ends.

BACK PERSONAL INITIATIVE WITH INTENSE ACTION

Organized Thinking is thought in motion. It requires three elements to be activated and working together: Definiteness of Purpose combined with personal initiative and backed by intense action. You will never achieve your major goals in life unless you get into the habit of doing what should be done without somebody telling you to do it. Another way of defining personal initiative might be the ability to see things as they are and do things as they should be done.

"Right here is where many men deceive themselves by believing they are organized thinkers," Carnegie tells us. "I have heard

Anyone may produce "miracles" by the simple process of taking possession of their own mind and directing it to definite ends.

not a few men say, 'I have been thinking of doing this or doing that, but so far I have found no way to do it.' The main weakness of such men consists in the fact that they have left out of their thinking one important factor–physical action expressed through Definiteness of Purpose."

The importance of action cannot be overstated. Action! Action! Action, and still more action! Let that word *action* burn itself into your consciousness, and you will begin to search for ways and means of organizing your thoughts through plans that enable the expression of action.

There must be action in making a start; action to impel the individual to keep on going after the start has been made, even though the going may be difficult; and action directed to making a new start if one is overtaken by temporary defeat.

To build a habit of Organized Thinking expressed through action, start making decisions one by one. Knowing what you want will help in making decisions, of course, because you can always judge whether or not the decision will contribute to the overall picture you hold of your life plan.

Organized thought is an irresistible force that is capable of making steppingstones out of the stumbling blocks of defeat.

How could anyone be permanently defeated who has acquired the ability to transmute every emotion, every feeling, every fear, and every worry into a positive driving force for the attainment of definite ends? And this is precisely what Organized Thinking enables one to do. It organizes all the faculties of the mind and conditions them for the expression of faith!

Carnegie tells us organized thought is the source of all spiritual and mental growth, provided it is expressed through action. "One does not grow spiritually or mentally by thought alone," he emphasizes. "Growth is the result of thought expressed through voluntary and definitely controlled habits of action."

Unless you become "action conscious" you will never become an organized thinker. You may think from morning until night, but you must put your thoughts into action or you will be only a daydreamer. You may theorize, but you will never build a bridge, or manage an industry successfully, or do whatever it is you are set upon doing, unless you acquire the habit of putting your theories to the test of trial through action.

Yes, there is power in thought, provided it is organized and directed to definite ends, in terms of intelligent action!

GO THE EXTRA MILE

Not only should you get in the habit of expressing organized thinking through action, but you should also practice the principle of *going the extra mile.* This entails rendering more and better service than is required of you–without being asked.

Most people do exactly what is required of them, or what they are paid to do, and no more. This approach is what guides people along the path of mediocrity. The road to success, on the other hand, is traveled by those individuals who look for ways to render useful service to others while accomplishing their goals.

Organized thought is an irresistible force that is capable of making steppingstones out of the stumbling blocks of defeat.

Make it a habit to do more and better work than you are paid to do.

Going the extra mile supports the achievement of your major goals by:

- Inspiring a mental state of positivity and enthusiasm that cannot be suppressed by challenges or adversity.
- Reinforcing a habit of continuous action so that you avoid the traps of procrastination and idleness.
- Enticing others to support your aims as they observe your dedication and benefit from your service.

Nothing will stand in the way of people who commit themselves wholeheartedly to finding ways to add value in all their endeavors, for they will build a foundation of self-confidence and enthusiasm that will keep them active in the pursuit of their Definite Major Purpose.

Make it a habit to do more and better work than you are paid to do, every single day in your life, and soon you will begin to see your progress accelerated and your results magnified.

The combined application of these principles of success, when they are supported by the principle of Accurate Thinking, constitutes organized thought of the highest order known to humankind. But remember, there can be no combined application of these principles without intense, continuous, and persistent action in carrying out your aims and purposes. These principles take on the quality of power only by their use. The application, moreover, must be not merely intermittent, but a controlled and regularly implemented habit.

Adopt as your watchword *Organized Thinking expressed by action*–action directed toward definite ends through *Controlled Attention*, the principle to which we turn next.

CHAPTER 6

SHARPEN YOUR FOCUS THROUGH CONTROLLED ATTENTION

The short span of years known as an "average lifetime" is too short to permit any individual to achieve noteworthy success in any calling without the concentration of his or her efforts behind a Definite Major Purpose.

The history of the lives of successful individuals reveals clearly that the most successful are those who have "placed all their eggs in one basket" and concentrated their major efforts upon the protection of that basket. They are known as individuals with "one-track minds" because they knew where they were going and needed but one track to enable them to get there. Andrew Carnegie understood the importance of focusing one's mental and physical efforts on one major purpose, which is why he is known for saying, "Put all your eggs in one basket and then watch that basket."

An important function of the principle of self-discipline–perhaps its most important function–is that of aiding individuals

"Put all your eggs in one basket and then watch that basket."

–Andrew Carnegie

in the development and maintenance of habits of thought that enable them to fix their entire attention upon a desired purpose and to hold it there until that purpose has been attained.

Success in all the higher brackets of individual achievement is attained by the application of thought-power, properly organized and directed to definite ends. And power, whether it be thought power or physical power, is attained by the concentration of energy!

The scientist concentrates her mind upon the search for the hidden facts and secrets of nature, and lo! The combined powers of the universe seem to cooperate to reveal them to her.

In business and in industry, the principle of concentration is the keynote of success.

William Wrigley, Jr., concentrated upon the manufacture of a five-cent package of chewing gum and lived to see an entire nation of people take up the habit of chewing gum, not to mention the fortune he accumulated for his efforts.

F. W. Woolworth concentrated upon the operation of five-and-dime stores and accumulated a great fortune from the sales of gadgets and trinkets in the low-priced merchandise field.

John D. Rockefeller concentrated upon the refining and sale of oil and made it yield him a fortune sufficient for the needs of ten thousand men.

Henry Ford concentrated upon the manufacture and distribution of a low-priced, dependable automobile and became the head of one of America's greatest industrial empires.

Madam Curie concentrated upon the discovery of the source of radium and kept her mind on that purpose until nature was forced to give up the secret of radium.

The signers of the Declaration of Independence concentrated upon the desire for liberty and personal freedom for the people of the United States, and concentrated so effectively that liberty and freedom may become the common property of all the people of the world.

Andrew Carnegie concentrated upon the manufacture and sale of steel and remained steadfast in his purpose until he ushered in the great steel age, which was destined to change, for the better, the living habits and the standard of living of the people of an entire nation. His efforts yielded him more money than he could give away during his lifetime.

Concentration on one's major purpose projects a clear picture of that purpose upon the subconscious section of the mind and holds it there until it is taken over by the subconscious and acted upon.

MENTAL DISCIPLINE

Controlled Attention is the act of coordinating all the faculties of the mind and directing their combined power to a given end. It is an act that can be attained only by the strictest sort of self-discipline.

Concentration on one's major purpose projects a clear picture of that purpose upon the subconscious section of the mind and holds it there until it is taken over by the subconscious and acted upon.

Controlled Attention is organized mind power!

As a matter of fact, one cannot control the attention and direct it to a given end without the supporting influence of well-developed habits of thought, and these are attainable only by self-discipline.

The philosophy of personal achievement does not tell you what you should desire. Instead, *it is the right and privilege of every individual to direct their thoughts and desires to ends of their own choosing.*

Controlled Attention places you in the way of attaining the Master Key to the power of the mind. It is a scientific method for contacting and drawing upon the greatest reservoir of Infinite Intelligence for the supply of all human needs.

Controlled Attention is organized mind power!

Controlled Attention leads to mastery in any type of human endeavor because it enables one to focus the powers of his mind upon the attainment of a definite objective and to keep it so directed at will. Controlled Attention is self-mastery of the highest order, for it is an accepted fact that individuals who control their own mind may control everything else that gets in their way.

EXPRESSING CONTROLLED ATTENTION THROUGH PRAYER

The way to Controlled Attention is through *prayer*–and prayer not in the sense of a passive request for assistance, but rather a confident proclamation of your purpose. Dr. Alexis Carrel, who devoted thirty-three years to scientific research at the Rockefeller Institute and is the author of *Man, the Unknown*, described prayer as follows:

"Prayer is a force as real as terrestrial gravity. As a physician, I have seen men, after all other therapy had failed, lifted out of disease and melancholy by the serene effect of prayer. It is the only power in the world that seems to overcome the so-called 'laws of nature'; the occasions on which prayer has dramatically done this have been termed 'miracles.' But a constant, quieter miracle takes place hourly in the hearts of men and women who have discovered that prayer supplies them with a steady flow of sustaining power in their daily lives.

"Too many people," Dr. Carrel continues, "regard prayer as a formalized routine of words, a refuge for weaklings, or a childish petition for material things. We sadly undervalue prayer when we conceive it in these terms, just as we should underestimate rain by describing it as something that fills the birdbath in our gardens. Properly understood, prayer is a mature activity indispensable to the fullest development of personality–the ultimate integration of man's highest faculties. Only in prayer do we achieve that complete and harmonious assembly of body, mind and spirit which gives the frail human reed its unshakable strength."

Yes, "miracles" do take place in the hearts of men when they learn how to control their attention and project their thoughts and desires through their subconscious minds for then they may

Only in prayer do we achieve that complete and harmonious assembly of body, mind and spirit which gives the frail human reed its unshakable strength.

The potentialities of the power of fixed attention through concentration are many.

draw freely upon the great reservoir of Infinite Intelligence, the source of all miracles.

Prayer may be expressed by concentration on a definite objective, by the strictest habits of self-discipline, through these factors:

- *Definiteness of Purpose*, the starting point of all achievement
- *Imagination*, through which the object of your purpose is illuminated and mirrored in the mind so clearly that its nature cannot be mistaken
- The emotion of *desire* turned on until it attains the proportion of a burning desire that will not be denied fulfillment
- *Faith* in the attainment of the purpose–attained by a belief in its realization that is so strong that you can see yourself already in possession of it
- The full force of the *willpower* applied continuously in support of faith
- The *subconscious mind* picks up the picture thus conveyed to it and carries it out to its logical conclusion by whatever practical means may be available, according to the nature of the purpose.

These are some of the factors which enter into the principle of concentration. *And they embrace the procedure followed in all prayers that produce positive results.* If any one of these factors is missing in prayer, the results are apt to be negative and therefore disappointing.

Effective concentration requires that *one's attention be fully controlled* and directed to a definite objective! And this is precisely the condition which must prevail in all effective prayers.

Now we begin to recognize that the principle of effective concentration is something more than a means of attaining material things–that it is an important factor by which we may attain the Master Key that unlocks the door to all riches.

Controlled Attention is attained through the six factors I have just mentioned. Attention that is not controlled and directed may be nothing more than idle curiosity. The word "controlled" is the key to the explanation of the difference between the two.

The potentialities of the power of fixed attention through concentration are many, but none of them is greater nor more important than that of concentration upon a Definite Major Purpose as the object of one's life goal.

Hidden in two words–Controlled Attention–is a strange power that is sufficient to enable you to remove all the self-imposed limitations that most people accept or set up in their own minds–limitations by which some are bound throughout their lives–and to enlist the universe to support your pursuit of a major purpose.

CHAPTER 7

HARNESS THE LAW OF HARMONIOUS ATTRACTION

At the end of our exploration of the path to purpose we encounter a law of nature that, if we can harness it, gives us momentum in our journey and removes obstacles that stand in our way. This law of nature is as fundamental and as powerful as gravity; it governs the way our life unfolds–the thoughts we have, the habits we adopt, the people with whom we become close, and the success we enjoy in life. This is the law of nature through which like attracts like, known as the *law of harmonious attraction.*

The law of harmonious attraction dictates that forces and things that are suited to the needs of another in the great scheme of life have a natural tendency to get together.

We see this law in operation in nature, as vegetation attracts the mineral and chemical elements of the soil and combines them with units of energy in the air so as to product everything that grows in the soil–the means by which all life is sustained.

Here we find no antagonism, no "fighting" among the elements of matter or units of energy. They do their work in response to the great law of harmonious attraction, without opposition among themselves.

With humans, the law manifests the same way–for good or for bad. When thoughts of a negative nature dominate in the mind, they attract to them more negative thoughts after their own kind, bringing along other individuals whose thoughts are destructive, and so on. The person with negative thought patterns thus invites more negativity into their life, so that they look around and say, "Everything is conspiring to work against me–I can't catch a break, I have no one I can trust, and I cannot obtain the success I envisioned for myself." And so it is; in this case, the law of harmonious attraction ensures that the negative energy broadcast from that individual is met with energy of the same kind, both from within the individual and without.

On the other hand, those individuals who have mastered the principles of this philosophy and have formed the habit of applying these principles in all of their relationships with other people are benefitted by the law of harmonious attraction by having conditioned their mind so it will attract to them only such people and material things as they desire. Moreover, they have eliminated from their own mind all conflicting emotions, such as fear, envy, greed, hatred, jealousy, and doubt, so that they can prepare their minds for the application of the principle of Controlled Attention.

Great achievements come from minds that are at peace with themselves!

The students of this philosophy who have mastered it and apply it daily know that it is costly to be forced to combat the unfriendly forces of other minds. They know it is fatal to their chance of success if they neglect to conquer the unfriendly forces of their own minds. Great achievements come from minds that are at peace with themselves!

Peace within one's mind is not a matter of luck, but it is a priceless possession that can be attained only by self-discipline based upon Controlled Attention.

CONDITIONING YOUR MIND FOR HARMONIOUS ATTRACTION

Now let us examine the method by which you may condition your mind so as to get the fullest benefit from the law of harmonious attraction.

1. Definiteness of Purpose

Through the application of this principle, you decide what is desired, create a plan for attaining it, and then proceed to concentrate the major portion of your thoughts and efforts toward the attainment of that end. Then, using Controlled Attention, you can impress your desires, aims, plans, and purposes upon your subconscious mind, where the law of harmonious attraction finds contact with them.

2. Applied Faith

By adopting a Definite Major Purpose and actively carrying out the object of your purpose, you thereby demonstrate faith in your ability to attain your objective. When you take this step, your mental attitude has become predominantly positive, many of the self-imposed limitations of fear, doubt, and discouragement have disappeared, and you have no room left in the mind for thoughts of failure. You are so busy carrying out the object of your major purpose that you have no time to hesitate or procrastinate–and you have no desire to do so.

3. Personal Initiative

Through the application of personal initiative, you organize plans for the attainment of your Definite Major Purpose; then you test those plans for soundness. By this time, you have a solid basis for your faith in the ultimate success of your plans; therefore, you move with self-reliance that practically defies opposition. You are no longer held back by fear, doubt, or indecision.

4. Self-Discipline

Through the application of this principle, all the emotions–both the positive and the negative emotions–are harnessed and brought under complete control, thus providing you with the means of guarding against expending your energy unnecessarily on negative emotions or unproductive actions. At this

Both the positive and the negative emotions are harnessed and brought under complete control, thus providing you with the means of guarding against expending your energy unnecessarily on negative emotions or unproductive actions.

point, your mind begins to function like a perfectly constructed machine, with no lost motion and no dissipation of energy, for you have acquired the ability to translate your emotions into a powerful driving force by which your Definite Major Purpose may be attained.

It is also at this point that you have begun to develop willpower, which enables you to bring all the departments of your mind under your complete control and make them work together for the attainment of your Definite Major Purpose.

You must either take charge of your mind and feed it with the type of food you wish to reproduce, or you must pay the penalty of having your mind taken over by the negative influences of your own environment. There is no compromise between these two circumstances. You either take possession of your own mind and direct it to the attainment of what you desire, or your mind takes possession of you and gives you whatever the circumstances of life hand out.

The choice, however, is within the control of every human being, and the very fact that the power of thought is the only thing over which any human being has been given the right of complete control is highly suggestive of the huge potentialities available through the exercise of this profound prerogative.

CONCLUSION

PURPOSE IS A VERB

As we have seen, the path to purpose is successfully traveled through the application of a combination of principles. No single principle will give you what you need to attain what you most desire in life–it is only through the application of several principles together that the mind harnesses the law of harmonious attraction and converts your thoughts into a rhythm of achievement. In so doing, it creates a power that cannot be identified as the result of any individual thought, a power that may be greater than all individual thoughts combined–such a power, for instance, as can be attained through faith or through the joining of minds in a mastermind association.

We know from observation and experience that when the following principles are combined in the mind, they produce mind power bordering upon the miraculous:

- Definiteness of Purpose
- Self-discipline, through control of the emotions
- Applied Faith

- Accurate Thinking
- Organized Thinking expressed through action
- Controlled Attention

Here is a combination of principles capable of producing sufficient power for the solution of practically every human problem. If you apply them diligently, you will create for yourself a life of intentionality, purpose, and mental freedom. If you neglect them, you will waste this amazing resource available to you–your own mind power–and prevent yourself from experiencing and enjoying all that your life could have been.

These principles need to be *applied* to generate power. Simply reading about them will not create results, though it will set the right thoughts in motion in your mind to get you started on your journey.

Also, it is important for you to appreciate and enjoy the journey. Do not treat your major purpose merely as an end goal; that is the object that is associated with your purpose. *Purpose is found in the pursuit* of worthy goals. It is in the daily actions that require intentionality, the minute-by-minute thoughts that offer to elevate your mind to greater heights, the seconds spent focused on what kind of person you most want to be and how that person would move through the world and approach the joys and challenges that are inevitably part of life.

This philosophy of success, and the seven steps outlined in this book, provide you with the fundamental building blocks to a life filled with meaning and significance.

This philosophy of success, and the seven steps outlined in this book, provide you with the fundamental building blocks to a life filled with meaning and significance.

If you have followed this philosophy, you now know what you want, and you have learned to think accurately in procuring it.

You have a Definite Major Purpose in life, and a plan for attaining it.

You have acquired self-reliance and faith sufficient for your every need.

You have given yourself immunity against all the subtle forces that are seeking to take away your ability to control your thoughts.

You have found peace and harmony within your own mind.

You have learned to accept all the circumstances of your life and to make the most of them.

And you have taken possession of your own mind power and have acquired the ability to direct that power to the attainment of your Definite Major Purpose in life.

You have therefore experienced a changed life that gives you the reins to your fate, so that you can determine the exact direction you will travel.

Remember, you do not have to accept from life anything short of what you want from it. You do not have to settle for anything less than the full realization of your purpose. You hold the Master Key to purpose in the way you create, organize, and direct your thoughts toward greater ends.

MY PATH TO PURPOSE
Journal

You have a Definite Major Purpose in life, and a plan for attaining it.

ABOUT NAPOLEON HILL

(1883-1970)

"Remember that your real wealth can be measured not by what you have–but by what you are."

In 1908, during a particularly down time in the U.S. economy and with no money and no work, Napoleon Hill took a job to write success stories about famous men. Although it would not provide much in the way of income, it offered Hill the opportunity to meet and profile the giants of industry and business–the first of whom was the creator of America's steel industry, multimillionaire Andrew Carnegie, who became Hill's mentor.

Carnegie was so impressed by Hill's perceptive mind that following their three-hour interview he invited Hill to spend the weekend at his estate so they could continue the discussion. During the course of the next two days, Carnegie told Hill that he believed any person could achieve greatness if they understood the philosophy of success and the steps required to achieve it.

"It's a shame," he said, "that each new generation must find the way to success by trial and error when the principles are really clear-cut."

Carnegie went on to explain his theory that this knowledge could be gained by interviewing those who had achieved greatness and then compiling the information and research into a comprehensive set of principles. He believed that it would take at least twenty years, and that the result would be "the world's first philosophy of individual achievement." He offered Hill the challenge–for no more compensation than that Carnegie would make the necessary introductions and cover travel expenses.

It took Hill twenty-nine seconds to accept Carnegie's proposal. Carnegie told him afterward that had it taken him more than sixty seconds to make the decision he would have withdrawn the offer, for "a man who cannot reach a decision promptly, once he has all the necessary facts, cannot be depended upon to carry through any decision he may make."

It was through Napoleon Hill's unwavering dedication that his book *Think and Grow Rich* was written and more than 80 million copies have been sold.